JUNIOR COOKBOOK

igloo

igloo

First published in 2007 by Igloo Books Ltd
Cottage Farm, Sywell, NN6 OBJ
www.igloo-books.co.uk

Some recipes in this book contain nuts.

ISBN: 978-184561-572-7
Printed in China
3 5 7 9 10 8 6 4 2 1

Project management: Toucan Books
Author: Jacqueline Bellefontaine
Design and layout: Leah Germann
Cover design: Gerald Behrendt
Editor: Theresa Bebbington
Photography: Andrew Sydenham © Toucan Books
Proofreader: Marion Dent

Contents

Introduction

Preparations

The recipes in this book are for you to make – on your own or with an adult helping. Whether or not you'll need help with a recipe will depend on your age and experience. If you want to make one of the recipes on your own, first get your parents' permission – but, of course, cooking with your mum or dad can be fun too.

MEASUREMENTS

There are several way to measure ingredients. You could weigh them with a set of scales and weights, or use a spring-type scale. The old-fashioned scales and weights are the most accurate, and they are now sold to give both metric and imperial measurements (your mum or dad might prefer imperial). The Americans and Australians often use measuring cups to measure ingredients for a recipe, and they can be easier to use than fiddling about with scales. If you don't have a proper set of measuring cups in your kitchen but would like to use them, ask your mum or dad to buy a set from a specialist kitchen shop.

Always use professional-type measuring spoons, cups, and jugs – these are a standard size. Never use a regular spoon from the kitchen drawer or a cup from the cupboard – the recipe won't come out right. For the same reason, stick to one type of measuring system when cooking a recipe. If you decide to use metric, for example, follow all the metric measurements. Never measure some things in metric and other things in imperial cups.

BEFORE YOU COOK CHECKLIST

- Always read the recipe completely through before you start, and have all the ingredients and the equipment you'll need ready.
- Ask for help when using a sharp knife or handling a hot dish if required. Look out for a knife or oven glove symbol.
- Tie your hair back if it's long, wash your hands and wear an apron.
- Wash all fruits and vegetables before you use them.
- Always check the "use by" and "best before" dates – never use food that is out of date or with signs of mold.
- Always use a separate chopping board and knife when cutting raw meat – never use it for vegetables.
- Always wash your hands after handling raw meat.
- Always use oven gloves or mitts when handling hot food or dishes.
- Never put hot dishes directly on the work surface – use a trivet, mat, or wooden board to protect the surface.
- Always put the handle of a saucepan on the hob to the side – it will be less likely to be knocked into this way.
- Always grip the handle of a pan on the hob firmly when stirring.

Measurements & Tips

MEASURING EQUIPMENT
In the "You'll Need" list we've listed "measuring equipment" as a general guideline because the type of equipment you'll need may sometimes depend on which measuring system you use. You'll need either some type of scales or American measuring cups. Decide on the measuring system you want to use before you choose the measuring equipment you'll need.

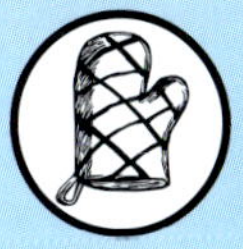

If you see an oven glove, the recipe involves heating food on the hob or in the oven.

A picture of a knife means you'll need to use a sharp knife to make the recipe.

COOKING TIPS

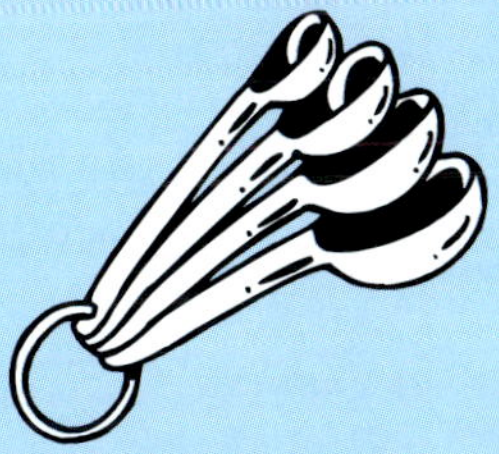

TO SOFTEN BUTTER, take it out of the refrigerator and let stand at room temperature for 10 to 15 minutes, or zap it in the microwave for a few seconds, but not too long – you don't want melted butter. If the butter gives slightly when pressed but does not crack, it's ready to use.

TO GREASE AND LINE A BAKING PANS first use a pencil to trace the shape of the tin on to the parchment. Use scissors to cut the parchment along the outline. Then grease the tin by rubbing it with butter or brushing on some oil with a pastry brush. Lay the parchment on the bottom of the tin.

WHEN USING MEASURING CUPS AND SPOONS for dry ingredients, always use the back of a knife to level off the ingredients – unless the recipe says to use a rounded spoon.

TO CRUSH GARLIC, use a garlic press. Remove a clove from the bulb and take off the skin – cutting off the ends with a cook's knife will make this easier. Then put the clove into the garlic press and squeeze the arms of the press together.

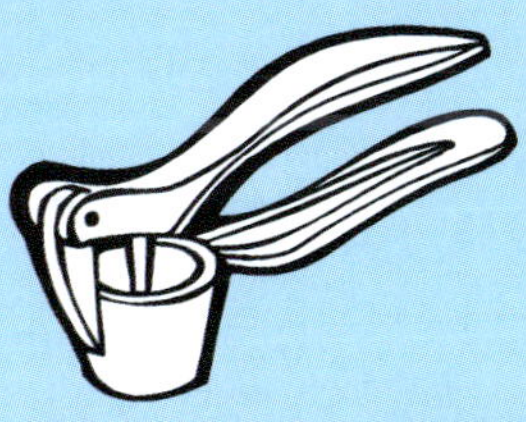

TO REMOVE THE CORE AND SEEDS FROM A BELL PEPPER, lie it on its side and cut down one side. Turn the pepper and keep cutting the sides, making sure you cut through where the core attaches to the walls of the pepper, until you've gone all the way around. Discard the top, with the core and seeds attached.

1

LET'S CELEBRATE

There are many reasons for family and friends to get together on special occasions to celebrate. These are sometimes the same around the world, but there are also customs and traditions that you may not know about. **LET'S CELEBRATE** is full of recipe ideas and advice on how you can join in on these wonderful celebrations!

Turn to pages **10–11** for **Sweet Corn Fritters & Pinwheel Sandwiches.** For **Wonky Jelly,** see pages **12–13.**

Birthday Party

Birthday Cake, Pinwheel Sandwiches, Sweet Corn Fritters, & Wonky Jello

Party Time! Your party is guaranteed to be a hit with this great cake and plenty of yummy snacks. All you need now are candles and friends!

BIRTHDAY CAKE

To write your name on the cake, save some chocolate frosting and use a narrow nozzle to pipe it out.

Serves: 4

YOU'LL NEED

Oven gloves
2 shallow 20cm/8in round cake pans
Greaseproof paper or nonstick baking parchment
Scissors
Oil or butter for greasing
Pastry brush
Measuring equipment
Sieve
2 mixing bowls
Hand-held electric mixer or wooden spoon
Cooling rack
Plate
Piping bag and small star nozzle
Metal spatula
Small bowl
Candles and holders

INGREDIENTS

225g/8oz/1½cups all-purpose flour
55g/2oz/½cup cocoa powder
1½ tsp baking powder
225g/8oz/1cup butter, softened
225g/8oz/1cup superfine sugar
4 eggs

For the butter cream:
150g/5oz/5 tbsp butter, softened
285g/10oz/2½cups confectioners' sugar
2 tbsp cocoa powder

To decorate:
Chocolate sprinkles
175g/6oz/1½cups confectioners' sugar
1–2 tbsp water
Sugar flowers or sweets

1. Preheat the oven to 180°C/350°F/Gas mark 4. Lightly grease and line the base of the pans.
2. With the sieve, sift the flour, cocoa powder, and baking powder into a bowl and add the butter, sugar and eggs. Beat together with a hand-held mixer or wooden spoon until smooth.
3. Divide the mixture between the two cake pans and level the surface.
4. Bake for 20 to 25 minutes in the center of the oven until springy to the touch. Allow to cool for 5 minutes, then transfer to a wire rack to cool completely.
5. Make the butter cream frosting by beating the butter until soft. Sift together the sugar and cocoa and gradually beat into the butter.
6. Use one-third of the butter cream frosting to sandwich the two cakes together. Spoon some of it into a piping bag fitted with the star nozzle and spread the remainder around the sides of the cake with the spatula. Place the sprinkles on a piece of baking parchment, then roll the sides of the cake in the sprinkles to coat. Place the cake on a plate.
7. Pipe the remaining butter cream around the edge of the cake.
8. Sift the confectioners' sugar into a bowl and slowly add enough water, a teaspoon at a time, to form a smooth frosting. Pour over the top of the cake and allow to set.
9. Decorate with the sugar flowers or sweets and arrange the candles and holders on the cake.

Birthday Party continued

SWEET CORN FRITTERS

Makes: about 20

YOU'LL NEED	INGREDIENTS
Measuring equipment	115g/4oz/1cup all-purpose flour
Food processor	½ tsp each paprika, ground coriander and cumin
Mixing bowl	1 egg
Cook's knife	85ml/3fl oz/⅓cup milk
Chopping board	½ red bell pepper
Large metal spoon	4 scallions
Large skillet	310g/11oz can sweet corn niblets
Draining spoon	Salt and freshly ground black pepper
Kitchen towel	Oil for frying
Plate	***To serve:***
	Sweet chilli sauce or ketchup

1. Place the flour and spices in a food processor. Add the egg and milk and blend until it forms a smooth, thick batter. Pour the mixture into a mixing bowl.
2. Remove the core and seeds from the red pepper and finely chop it with a cook's knife. Trim the ends off the scallions and slice them.
3. Stir the pepper, onions, and sweet corn into the batter with a spoon.
4. Ask an adult to help you with the cooking. Heat 1cm/½in oil in a skillet. Drop in a few dessert spoonfuls of the fritter mixture into the oil and cook for 4 to 6 minutes, turning once. Remove the fritters from the pan with a draining spoon, drain them on kitchen paper and put them in a warm oven while you repeat with the remaining mixture.
5. Serve as a starter or light snack with a little sweet chilli sauce or ketchup for dipping.

PINWHEEL SANDWICHES

Serves: 4–8

YOU'LL NEED	INGREDIENTS
Measuring equipment	4 medium-thick slices white or wholemeal bread
Bread knife	85g/3oz/⅓cup cream cheese
Chopping board	2 thin slices ham
Cook's knife	2 tbsp chopped fresh parsley (optional)
Rolling pin	1 tbsp finely chopped bell pepper (optional)
Small bowl	
Wooden spoon	
Dinner knife	
Plastic wrap	

1. Cut the crusts off the bread with the bread knife and flatten each slice slightly with a rolling pin.
2. Using the cook's knife, chop the ham into small pieces and beat it into the cream cheese with a wooden spoon. Beat in the parsley or pepper if you are using them.
3. Spread the cream-cheese mixture over the bread slices with a dinner knife. Starting at one side, roll up the bread tightly like a Swiss roll. Wrap it in plastic wrap and chill for 1 hour.
4. To serve, remove the rolls from the plastic wrap and cut into slices.

WONKY JELLO

Jello is always popular at a party. To make them a little special these jellos are set at a wonky angle – your friends will appreciate the extra effort.

Serves: 6–8

YOU'LL NEED	INGREDIENTS
Measuring equipment	150g/5oz package strawberry jello
Kettle	18–24 small strawberries
6 to 8 glasses	150g/5oz package lemon or lime jello
Tray	120ml/4fl oz/½cup whipping cream
Mixing bowl	Candy sprinkles
Balloon whisk or hand-held electric mixer	
Spoon	

GET IT STRAIGHT!
If you find getting the jello to set on a slant is a bit too difficult, let the jello set straight as normal. To make it look extra special try making stripes. Pour in three or more layers of jello – but allow each layer to set before adding the next layer.

1. Break the strawberry jello into cubes and place them in a measuring jug.
2. Bring a kettle of water to the boil and pour into the jug to the 300ml/10fl oz mark. Stir until the jello dissolves, then add enough cold water to make 600ml/20fl oz.
3. You'll need two strawberries for each glass. Remove their stems and put them in the glasses. Pour some jello into each glass so that all the glasses are half full. Any leftover jello can be put into small dishes to enjoy another time.
4. Now comes the tricky bit. When the jello has cooled down place it into the fridge at a jaunty angle. To do this find something to prop up the glasses at a slant. Place the glasses in a tray with sides, with the bottom of the glasses resting against one side of the tray, and prop up the glasses. A little poster putty may help to hold them in place. Carefully place them in the fridge and chill until set. Take care when opening the fridge that the glasses do not slip.
5. When the strawberry jello has set, make up the lemon or lime jello in the same way as before.
6. When the lemon or lime jello is cold stand the glasses up straight and pour in the second jello to almost fill the glasses. Chill them in the fridge until the jello has set.
7. Finally, lightly whip the cream with the whisk and pile it on top of the jello. Decorate with the remaining strawberries and sprinkles.

Happy New Year

French Bread Pizza & No Cook Chocolate Bar

YOU'LL NEED	INGREDIENTS
Oven mitts	1 small French bread baton
Measuring equipment	8 tbsp tomato pizza topping
Bread knife	30g/1oz/1cup mushrooms
Dinner knife	55g/2oz pepperoni
Cook's knife	85g/3oz/¾cup yellow cheese
Chopping board	55g/2oz/½cup mozzarella cheese
Grater	

FRENCH BREAD PIZZA

This recipe is easy to change. You can replace the pepperoni and mushrooms with chopped ham and pineapple chunks before adding the cheese. Or replace the yellow cheese with Cheddar cheese.

Serves: 4

1. Preheat the broiler. Cut the bread in half, using the bread knife, then split them in two. Toast the bread under the broiler, with the cut sides facing up, until golden.

2. Spread the toasted sides with the tomato topping. Using a cook's knife, slice the mushrooms and arrange them on the topping. Thinly slide the pepperoni and also arrange them on the topping.

3. Grate the yellow cheese and dice the mozzarella cheese. Scatter them over the top of your pizzas.

4. Place the pizzas under the broiler and cook them until the cheese melts. Allow the pizzas to cool for a few moments before serving them.

NEW YEAR'S BANG!
Fireworks are often set off at midnight. You can create your own noise and fun with streamers, horns and rattles. And don't forget to make a resolution – this tradition dates back to the early Babylonians!

BRINGING IN THE NEW YEAR

In many countries the start of a new year is celebrated at midnight. The next day family and friends get together to continue the celebration. Whether you enjoy these snacks at midnight or have them on New Year's Day, they will be a hit with family and friends.

NO COOK CHOCOLATE BAR

Makes: 12

YOU'LL NEED	INGREDIENTS
Oven mitts	85g/3oz/½cup mixed dried fruits
Measuring equipment	55g/2oz/1cup mini marshmallows
18cm/7in square cake pan	16 graham crackers
Greaseproof paper or baking parchment	200g/7oz plain chocolate
Oil/pastry brush or butter for greasing	55g/2oz/4 tbsp butter
Mixing bowl	
Small heatproof bowl	
Small saucepan	
Wooden spoon	
Cook's knife	

1. Grease and line the base of the cake pan with the baking parchment.
2. Place the fruits and marshmallows in the mixing bowl. Break the biscuits into small pieces, taking care not to crush them, and add them to the bowl.
3. Break the chocolate into squares and place in a small heatproof bowl with the butter. With an adult's help, place the bowl over a pan of gently simmering water and stir until melted. Or, cook in a microwave at 50 per cent for 1 to 2 minutes and stir to combine.
4. Using oven mitts – the bowl will be hot – pour the chocolate over the biscuit mixture and stir until it is coated in the chocolate mixture.
5. Pour the mixture into the pan and press down well. Put it in the refrigerator and chill until it sets.
6. To serve, carefully remove the mixture from the tin and cut it into 12 pieces, using a cook's knife.

A ROMANTIC DAY

St Valentine's Day occurs every February 14th and is named for a Roman priest who married couples in secret – at the time marriages were banned so the emperor could recruit soldiers.

St Valentine's Day

Valentine Cookies & Strawberry Smoothie

VALENTINE COOKIES

Makes: about 30

YOU'LL NEED

- Oven mitts
- 2 baking sheets
- A little oil or butter for greasing
- Pastry brush
- Measuring equipment
- Large mixing bowl
- Dinner knife
- Rolling pin
- Heart-shaped cookie cutter
- Cooling rack
- Small mixing bowl
- Metal spoon
- Metal spatula
- Sieve

INGREDIENTS

- 175g/6oz/1½cups all-purpose flour, plus extra for dusting
- 2 tbsp ground rice
- 115g/4oz/½cup butter
- 55g/2oz/¼cup confectioners' sugar
- 1–2 tbsp cold water

To decorate:

- 175g/6oz/¾cup confectioners' sugar
- About 6 tsp cold water
- Pink food coloring
- Sugar sprinkles

THE NAME GAME!
Try writing your friend's name on a cookie – or if you know it, her secret admirer's name.

1. Preheat the oven to 200°C/400°F/Gas mark 6. Lightly grease two baking sheets.
2. Place the flour and ground rice in a large bowl. Cut the butter into small pieces and rub them into the flour and rice with your fingers until the mixture looks like fine breadcrumbs. Mix in the confectioners' sugar. Add 1 tbsp of water and use your hands to form a soft dough. Add a little extra water if it seems dry. Chill for 20 minutes.
3. On a work surface with a little flour dusted over it, roll out the dough until it is about 6mm/¼in thick. Cut out the cookies using a cookie cutter. Place them on the baking sheets and bake for 8 to 10 minutes until crisp and golden.
4. Allow the cookies to cool on the baking sheet for 2 to 3 minutes, then transfer them to a wire rack to cool completely.
5. To make the frosting, sift the superfine sugar into a bowl, add a few drops of food coloring and stir in 1 tbsp of water. Add water, a tsp at a time, until the frosting is smooth. Spread it over the tops of the cookies and decorate with the sprinkles if you wish, then let them set.

STRAWBERRY SMOOTHIE

Serves: 4

YOU'LL NEED

- Measuring equipment
- Food processor or liquidizer
- Cook's knife
- Chopping board
- Glasses

INGREDIENTS

- 18 strawberries
- 225g/8oz/1cup plain yogurt
- 600ml/20fl oz/2½cups milk
- 4 tbsp honey or confectioners' sugar
- Ice cubes

1. Put 4 small strawberries to one side and place the remaining strawberries, yogurt, milk, and honey or confectioners' sugar in a food processor or liquidizer and whiz them until they are frothy and well blended.
2. Place three or four ice cubes into each of the 4 glasses, and divide the smoothie between the glasses. Using the cook's knife, make a cut in the bottom of the 4 strawberries and slip them on to the glass rims.

TIP!
Practise piping a shamrocks on to a plate or baking parchment before you pipe them on to the cupcakes. But relax – the shamrocks don't need to be perfect.

St Patrick's Day

Shamrock Cakes

Irish people around the world celebrate St Patrick's Day on March 17th, the day that St Patrick died. The three-leafed shamrock is linked with St Patrick because he used it to teach people about the Father, Son, and Holy Spirit. Nowadays, St Patrick's Day is remembered by parades – and, of course, wearing something green.

SHAMROCK CAKES

The two-tone green-and-white insides of these cupcakes will surprise your friends when they take their first bite.

Makes: 18

YOU'LL NEED	INGREDIENTS
Oven mitts	115g/4oz/1cup all-purpose flour
Measuring equipment	1 tsp baking powder
2 muffin pans	115g/4oz/½cup butter, softened
18 paper muffin cases	115g/4oz/½cup castor sugar
Sieve	2 eggs
2 mixing bowls	Green food coloring
Hand-held electric mixer or wooden spoon	***For decorating:***
2 small bowls	225g/8oz/2cups confectioners' sugar
2 metal spoons	About 2tbsp water
Cooling rack	Green food coloring
Dinner knife	
Small piping bag	
Writing nozzle	

MAKE A SHAMROCK BADGE!
Wear a shamrock on St Patrick's Day. To make your own badge cut a piece of card into a shamrock shape and attach a safety pin to the back with Sellotape. Paint it green and glue on some glitter.

1. Preheat the oven to 180°C/350°F/Gas mark 4. Line the muffin pans with the paper cases.

2. Using the sieve, sift the flour and baking powder into the mixing bowl. Add the butter, sugar, and eggs. Beat together with a hand-held mixer or wooden spoon until just smooth.

3. Divide the mixture into two and add a little green food coloring to one portion. Using two small spoons, place a spoonful of green cake mixture and a spoonful of white cake mixture into each paper case.

4. Bake in the center of the oven for 15 minutes until the cakes are springy to the touch. Allow them to cool for 5 minutes, then transfer to a wire rack to cool properly.

5. To decorate, sift the confectioners' sugar into a bowl and slowly add enough water to mix to a smooth frosting. Put aside about 1 rounded tbsp of the frosting, and spread the remaining frosting over the top of the cakes.

6. Add a little green food coloringto the remaining frosting and spoon it into a piping bag fitted with a writing nozzle. Pipe a shamrock-shaped leaf on the top of each cake. Allow the frosting to set.

At Easter Christians remember the death and resurrection of Jesus. However, many Easter traditions are linked with the worship of the pagan goddess Eastre, such as giving colored eggs as gifts, the notion of the Easter rabbit and wearing new clothes. This last custom is now enjoyed during the Easter parade and by wearing Easter bonnets!

EASTER NESTS

These fun nests are easy to make – your younger brothers or sisters will love helping you make them.

Makes: about 14

YOU'LL NEED	INGREDIENTS
Measuring equipment	55g/2oz/4 tbsp butter
Large saucepan	115g/4oz milk chocolate
Wooden spoon	3 tbsp corn syrup
Paper muffin cases	2 tbsp cocoa powder
Tray	100g/3½oz/4cups puffed rice cereal
Metal spoon	***To decorate:*** Mini chocolate Easter eggs

1. Put the butter, chocolate, syrup, and cocoa powder in a saucepan and heat gently, stirring with a wooden spoon until melted and well combined.
2. Remove the pan from the heat and stir in the puffed rice cereal until it is well coated.
3. Place the muffin cases on a tray and spoon the chocolate mixture into them, using a metal spoon. Make a dip in the center so that they form "nests".
4. Chill the nests in the fridge until they set.
5. Arrange the eggs inside the nests.

DESIGNER EGGS!

Before dyeing a hard-boiled egg, wrap a rubber band around it or put star- or heart-shaped stickers on it. Dye the egg, then remove the rubber band or stickers to reveal the pattern. Or use a crayon to write or draw on the egg – the dye won't stick to the crayon.

TIP!

You can create your own Easter bonnet with a plain straw hat (buy one from a craft shop). With a grownup's help, use a glue gun to attach fake flowers, ribbons, bows and Easter decorations – or anything that might be fun! No straw hat? Try decorating a paper plate. Make two holes for yarn to tie it under your chin.

Turn to pages **24-25** for **Easy Pasta Supper.** The **Special Lemon Drizzle Cake** recipe is on pages **26-27.**

Mother's Day

Dips and Sticks, Easy Pasta Supper, & Special Lemon Drizzle Cake

A day to be remembered! Mothering Sunday occurs in Britain on the fourth Sunday of Lent (the 40 days before Easter). In the United States, Australia and some European countries, Mother's Day is on the second Sunday in May. Prepare this meal on Mother's Day, but keep it a secret to give your mom a real surprise.

DIPS & STICKS

Serve these as a starter or a healthy snack.

Serves: 4

YOU'LL NEED

- Measuring equipment
- Can opener
- Food processor
- Spoon
- Mixing bowl
- Wooden spoon
- Grater
- 2 small serving bowls
- Cook's knife
- Chopping board
- Vegetable peeler

INGREDIENTS

For the tuna dip:

- 200g/7oz can tuna in spring water
- 1 tbsp lemon juice
- 115g/4oz/½cup mayonnaise
- Salt and freshly ground pepper

For the cheesy dip:

- 85g/3oz/⅓cup cream cheese
- 85g/3oz/⅓cup plain yogurt
- 30g/1oz/¼cup Monterey Jack cheese

To serve:

- A variety of vegetables such as bell pepper, celery, cucumber, and carrots

1. Open the can of tuna and drain away the liquid. Put the tuna, lemon juice, mayonnaise, and the seasonings in a food processor and whiz until smooth. Transfer the mixture to a small serving bowl.

2. Using a wooden spoon, beat together the cream cheese and yogurt until it forms a smooth mixture. Using the grater, grate the cheese, then beat the cheese into the mixture with the spoon. Transfer the mixture to a small serving bowl.

3. Wash and prepare all the vegetables, removing the core and seeds from the bell pepper with a cook's knife, peeling the carrots with a vegetable peeler and trimming the vegetables as required. Using the knife, cut the vegetables into stick shapes.

4. Arrange the vegetables and serve them with the dips.

FINISHING DETAILS!
To make this starter extra special for mom, stand the vegetable sticks up in a pretty glass or arrange them in a fun pattern on a colorful plate.

Mother's Day continued

EASY PASTA SUPPER

Give your mom the night off by making this easy – and tasty – supper dish.

Serves: 4

YOU'LL NEED

- Cook's knife
- Chopping board
- Garlic press
- Small saucepan
- Wooden spoon
- Large saucepan
- Colander

INGREDIENTS

- 1 onion
- 150g/5oz/1¼cups button mushrooms
- 2 cloves garlic
- 2 tbsp olive oil
- 400g/14oz can chopped tomatoes
- 2 tbsp tomato purée
- 1 tsp dried oregano
- Salt and freshly ground black pepper
- 350g/12oz pasta

To serve:

Grated Parmesan cheese

A FLAKY TREAT!
For the freshest flavr, buy ungrated Parmesan cheese and make large flakes using a wide slot in the grater.

1. Using a cook's knife, peel and chop the onion and slice the mushrooms. Crush the garlic with a garlic press.
2. Heat the oil in a small saucepan and fry the onion for 3 to 4 minutes until it softens, stirring occasionally with the wooden spoon. Stir in the mushrooms and garlic and cook for another 3 minutes.
3. Add the tomatoes, tomato purée, and oregano and bring to the boil. Reduce the heat and simmer gently for 10 minutes until slightly thickened. Season with the salt and pepper.
4. Meanwhile, cook the pasta in the large saucepan in lightly salted, boiling water for 10 minutes or as directed on the packet.
5. Drain the pasta in the colander. Add the pasta back to the large saucepan, top with the sauce and toss to coat the pasta with the sauce. Serve with Parmesan cheese.

TIP!
If you don't serve **Dips & Sticks** as a starter (see pages **22–23**), you can make the pasta supper dish more filling by adding a chopped courgette to the sauce when you add the tomatoes in step 3.

TIP!
Instead of the petals you can use soft fruits such as redcurrants, strawberries, or raspberries to decorate the cake. Brush them with the egg white and dust with sugar.

Mother's Day continued

SPECIAL LEMON DRIZZLE CAKE

This pretty cake is really easy to make. With this and the other recipes, don't forget to do the washing up and clean up any mess so that your mom won't have to.

Serves: 8–10

YOU'LL NEED

- Oven mitts
- Measuring equipment
- 23cm/9in ring tin
- A little oil or butter for greasing
- 2 pastry brushes
- Grater
- Cook's knife
- Chopping board
- Lemon squeezer
- Sieve
- Large mixing bowl
- Hand-held electric mixer or wooden spoon
- Dinner knife
- 2 cooling racks
- Balloon whisk
- 2 small mixing bowls
- Metal spoon
- Plate

INGREDIENTS

- 1 lemon
- 225g/8oz/2cups all-purpose flour
- 1½tsp baking powder
- 225g/8oz/1cup butter, softened
- 225g/8oz/1cup fine sugar
- 4 eggs

To decorate:

- 1 egg white
- Fine sugar
- Rose petals
- 150g/5oz/1¼cups confectioners' sugar
- 1 tbsp lemon juice

FLOWERS FOR MOM!
Serve this cake either for dessert or for afternoon tea. You can decorate the table with a flowered tablecloth and fresh flowers from the garden.

1. Preheat the oven to 180°C/350°F/Gas mark 4. Lightly grease the tin with a little oil.
2. Using a grater, grate the zest (the colored part of the peel) from the lemon, taking care not to include the white pith. Cut the lemon in half and squeeze out the juice with the lemon squeezer.
3. Using a sieve, sift the flour and baking powder into a mixing bowl and add the butter, sugar, eggs, lemon zest, and juice. Beat together with a hand-held mixer or wooden spoon until just smooth.
4. Pour the batter into the ring tin and level the top with a dinner knife. Bake for 35 to 40 minutes until firm to the touch. Allow the cake to cool for 5 minutes, then remove from the tin and transfer to a wire rack to cool.
5. Meanwhile, prepare the decorations. Lightly whisk the egg white until just frothy with a balloon whisk. Put some superfine sugar on a plate. Brush the rose petals with a little egg white, then dust with superfine sugar. Place on a wire rack to dry.
6. When the cake is cold, sift the confectioners' sugar into a bowl and slowly add the lemon juice and mix with a spoon to form a smooth runny frosting.
7. Spread the frosting over the top of the cake with the spoon, allowing it to dribble down the sides a little. Arrange the rose petals on top. Allow the frosting to set before serving. Store in a cool dry place.

You can find recipes for **Confetti Rice Salad** on pages **30–31.**

Father's Day

Really Great Burgers & Confetti Rice Salad

A day for your dad. Father's Day was first celebrated in the United States on June 19th and today it is celebrated there and elsewhere on the third Sunday of June. Dad can light the barbecue while you make this tempting feast for him. Plan something else to help him relax. He may enjoy a crossword or word-search puzzle – you can make one especially for him.

REALLY GREAT BURGERS

You can prepare these burgers, then ask a grownup to cook them on the barbecue.

Serves: 4

YOU'LL NEED

- Measuring equipment
- Mixing bowl
- Cook's knife
- Chopping board
- Metal spatula

INGREDIENTS

- 600g/1lb 5oz lean ground beef
- 1 tsp mild or hot chilli powder (optional)
- Salt and freshly ground black pepper
- 1 large beefsteak tomato
- 4 burger buns
- A few lettuce leaves

To serve:

- Pickles
- Ketchup
- Mayonnaise
- Mustard

JUST FOR DAD!
Let your dad know that he's special by making him a paper crown and crowning him king for the day!

1. Put the meat into the mixing bowl, add the chilli powder if using and season with the salt and pepper. Using your hands, squish the meat mixture between your fingers to thoroughly mix in the seasoning.
2. Divide the meat into four. Shape the portions into balls, then press down to flatten them into burger shapes.
3. Using a cook's knife, cut the tomato into four slices – place the tomato on its side and cut the slices parallel with the top. Put the pickles into a small dish and get the ketchup, mayonnaise, and mustard ready to serve.
4. Ask a grownup to cook the burgers for 5 minutes on each side, either on a barbecue over medium-hot coals or under a grill. Add the tomato slices for the last minute, turning them once.
5. Slice the buns in half and toast the cut side until pale golden.
6. Serve the burgers with some lettuce in the toasted buns, topped with the tomato. Provide the pickles and other condiments so that each diner can help themselves.

Father's Day continued

CONFETTI RICE SALAD

Prepare this salad several hours ahead of time and keep it in the refrigerator to allow the rice to absorb the flavors. Serve it at room temperature or chilled.

Serves: 4

YOU'LL NEED

- Measuring equipment
- Large saucepan
- Wooden spoon
- Sieve
- Cook's knife
- Chopping board
- Large mixing bowl
- Small bowl
- Fork

INGREDIENTS

- 275g/10oz/1½cups easy cook, long-grain rice
- 4 scallions
- 1 green bell pepper
- 1 red bell pepper
- 4 rings tinned pineapple
- 6 tbsp sweet corn niblets

For the dressing:

- 3 tbsp pineapple juice
- 3 tbsp olive oil
- 2 tbsp white wine vinegar
- 1 tsp wholegrain mustard
- Salt and freshly ground black pepper

DON'T LIKE PINEAPPLE?
Instead of the pineapple, you can add 2 carrots, diced and boiled for 8 minutes – let the carrots cool before adding them in step 3, and replace the pineapple juice in the dressing with apple juice.

1. Bring a large saucepan of water to the boil and add the rice, stir with a wooden spoon, reduce the heat, and cook for 15 minutes or until the rice is just tender. Drain in a sieve and run under cold water until the rice is cold. Drain well.
2. Using a cook's knife, trim the ends off the scallions and slice them. Remove and discard the core and seeds from the bell peppers, then cut the peppers into small pieces. Cut the pineapple into bite-sized pieces.
3. Mix the rice, onions, peppers, pineapple, and sweet corn together in the large bowl.
4. Place the ingredients for the dressing in a small bowl, and whisk them together with a fork until well combined.
5. Pour the dressing over the rice and toss together until all the vegetables and pineapple are well coated with the dressing.

TIP!
The recipes for Father's Day are ideal for a day out at a picnic area with a barbecue. Prepare the burgers the night before and the kebabs in the morning, but don't cook them – wrap them up in plastic wrap or foil. Also prepare the rice salad. Cook the burgers and kebabs at lunch time on the barbecue.

To find the recipe for **Witches' Broomsticks,** turn to pages **34–35.** You'll find **Spider Web Cookies** on pages **36–37.**

Halloween

Starry Pumpkin Soup, Witches' Broomsticks, & Spider Web Cookies

Have a scary night! The Celts first dressed up in costumes to avoid spirits on October 31st, and trick-or-treating began with Catholics asking for food for the poor on All Hallows' Day on November 1st. Start off a Halloween with your friends with these yummy treats before the evening activities.

STARRY PUMPKIN SOUP

Serve this traditional soup with fun star-shaped croutons – small pieces of toasted bread.

Serves: 6–8

YOU'LL NEED

- Measuring equipment
- Cook's knife
- Chopping board
- Large saucepan
- Wooden spoon
- Food processor or liquidizer
- Small star-shaped cookie cutters

INGREDIENTS

- 4 tbsp olive oil
- 500g/1lb 2oz/4½cups pumpkin flesh
- 1 onion
- 1 clove garlic
- 750ml/25fl oz/3cups vegetable stock
- 150ml/5fl oz/¾cup heavy cream (optional)
- Salt and freshly ground black pepper
- ¼ tsp freshly grated nutmeg

For the star croutons:

- 2 slices white or wholemeal bread
- A little vegetable oil

1. Ask an adult to cut the pumpkin, remove its flesh and cut the flesh into cubes. With a cook's knife, peel and chop the onion and garlic.
2. Heat the oil in a large saucepan and fry the pumpkin, onion, and garlic over a low heat for 5 to 10 minutes, stirring occasionally with a wooden spoon, until softened.
3. Add the stock. Cover with a lid and simmer for 30 minutes. Remove the pan from the heat and allow the mixture to cool.
4. Pour the soup into a food processor or liquidizer and whiz until smooth. Return the soup to the pan and reheat slowly.
5. Meanwhile, cut star shapes from the bread, using a small cookie cutter. Toast them under a broiler until pale golden, turning once.
6. When the soup is piping hot, turn off the heat and stir in the cream. Season to taste with the salt and pepper and add the nutmeg. Serve the soup in warm bowls with the star croutons scattered on top.

WITCHES' BROOMSTICKS

These broomsticks are delicious cheesy biscuits that are fun to make and eat. For other occasions you can cut the pastry into rectangles and serve the biscuits with other types of soup.

Makes: about 24

YOU'LL NEED

- Oven mitts
- Measuring equipment
- Baking sheet
- A little oil or butter for greasing
- Pastry brush
- Mixing bowl
- Dinner knife
- Wooden spoon
- Rolling pin
- Cook's knife
- Cooling rack

INGREDIENTS

- 225g/8oz/2cups all-purpose flour
- 115g/4oz/½cup butter
- 115g/4oz/1cup yellow cheese, finely grated
- About 5 tbsp milk

OTHER SHAPES!

Instead of using all of the dough to make broomsticks, use some of it to cut out pumpkin shapes with scary faces. Or try making pointy witches' hats with a brim. Cut tall triangles for the main part of the hat but make the bottom part rounded. Then cut curved brims and attach them as described in step 6 to the other part of the hats.

1. Preheat the oven to 200°C/400°F/Gas mark 6. Lightly grease a baking sheet.
2. Put the flour in a mixing bowl. Cut the butter into small cubes with a dinner knife and add it to the flour. Using your fingertips, rub the butter into the flour until the mixture resembles fine breadcrumbs.
3. Stir in the cheese with a wooden spoon, make a well in the center and add 4 tbsp of the milk. Mix to form a soft dough, adding a little extra milk if required.
4. Take about one-third of the dough and roll it out to form a 18x15cm/7x6in rectangle. Cut it in half lengthways, then cut each piece into 12 long strips. Place the strips on the baking sheet, making sure you leave plenty of space between them.
5. Roll out the remaining pastry to a 30x20cm/12x8in rectangle and cut this into 12.5cm/2in squares. Then cut each square in half to form two triangles.
6. Dampen one end of each stick with a dab of water and press a triangle of pastry on to the end. Using the cook's knife, cut lines into the triangle to make the bristles of the broom.
7. Bake the broomsticks for 10 to 12 minutes until they are golden and crisp. Allow them to cool on the tray for about 5 minutes before carefully transferring them to a wire rack to cool completely.

SPIDER WEB COOKIE

These spooky cookies are a sweet treat – why not enjoy a few of them before you go out trick-or-treating.

Makes: about 24

YOU'LL NEED

- Oven mitts
- Measuring equipment
- Hand-held electric mixer or wooden spoon
- Mixing bowl
- 3 small bowls
- Baking sheet
- Oil/pastry brush or butter for greasing
- Cook's knife
- Cooling rack
- Sieve
- Metal spoon
- Piping bag
- Small plain nozzle
- Dinner knife
- Cocktail stick

INGREDIENTS

175g/6oz/¾cup butter, softened
85g/3oz/¾cup confectioners' sugar
2 tbsp cocoa powder
225g/8oz/2cups all-purpose flour

To decorate:

175g/6oz/1½cups confectioners' sugar
1–2 tbsp orange juice
1 tsp cocoa powder

GHOULISH GATHERING!
While enjoying your Halloween meal with friends, why not start a scary story and have each guest add to it until it reaches a frightening ending.

1. Using a hand-held mixer or wooden spoon, beat together the butter and confectioners' sugar in a mixing bowl until light and fluffy.
2. With the sieve, sift the cocoa powder and flour together into a bowl, then gradually beat them into the butter mixture. Use your fingers to add the last of the flour mixture. Roll the dough into a log shape and chill for 30 minutes.
3. Preheat the oven to 180°C/350°F/Gas mark 4. Lightly grease the baking sheet. Using a cook's knife, cut the log into thin slices and place them on the baking sheet, leaving plenty of space between the slices.
4. Bake for 10 minutes until just firm. Leave the cookies to cool on the sheet for a few minutes before transferring them to a wire rack to cool completely.
5. To decorate, sift the icing sugar into a small bowl and gradually stir in the orange juice, a teaspoon at a time, until you have a smooth frosting. Spoon about 2 rounded tbsp into another bowl and beat in the cocoa powder and a little extra orange juice to make a smooth chocolate frosting. Spoon the chocolate frosting into a small piping bag.
6. Spread the light-colored frosting over each biscuit with a dinner knife and pipe spirals of chocolate frosting on top. While the frosting is still wet drag a cocktail stick through it from the center of the biscuit to the edge a few times to form a web. Serve after the frosting has set.

Home-made Cranberry Sauce & **Turkey Sandwich** are on pages **40–41.**

Thanksgiving

Pecan Pie, Home-made Cranberry Sauce, & Turkey Sandwich

A time to give thanks. The first American Thanksgiving in 1621 was a dinner held by the pilgrims to thank their Native American neighbors for their help. Since 1863 Thanksgiving has been celebrated on the last Thursday of November. Turkey is usually served for dinner, along with stuffing, cranberry sauce, and lots of side dishes.

PECAN PIE

Help mom out at Thanksgiving by making this popular American pie. You can make it a few weeks beforehand and freeze it until needed.

Serves: 6–8

YOU'LL NEED

- Oven mitts
- Mixing bowl
- Wooden spoon
- Small mixing bowl
- Fork

INGREDIENTS

- 2 tbsp plus 2 tsp corn syrup
- 55g/2oz/¼cup light muscovado sugar
- 1½tsp cornflour
- ½tsp vanilla extract
- 2 eggs
- 20cm/8in cooked pastry case
- 75g/3oz/¾cup pecan nuts

1. Preheat the oven to 190°C/375°F/Gas mark 5.
2. Using a wooden spoon, mix together the golden syrup, sugar, cornflour, and vanilla extract in the mixing bowl.
3. Place the eggs in a small bowl and beat with a fork, then gradually beat the beaten eggs into the sugar mixture.
4. Scatter or arrange the pecan nuts in the pastry case and pour in the filling.
5. Bake for 10 minutes, then reduce the oven temperature to 170°C/325°F/Gas mark 3 and bake for a further 15 to 20 minutes, until the filling is just set and golden brown. The filling will still be quite wobbly but it will firm up when cold.

THE FINISHING TOUCH!
You can serve a slice of pie with a scoop of vanilla ice cream – but first allow some time to let your dinner settle.

Thanksgiving continued

HOME-MADE CRANBERRY SAUCE

Cranberry sauce is simple to make. Cook up a batch for Thanksgiving dinner or to use for leftovers, including the Turkey Sandwich recipe.

Makes: 175g/6oz/1½cups

YOU'LL NEED	INGREDIENTS
Small saucepan	150g/5oz/1¼cups cranberries
Wooden spoon	4 tbsp orange juice
Small, air-tight plastic food container	2 tbsp superfine sugar

1. Place the ingredients in a saucepan and cook over a low heat for 10 to 15 minutes until the cranberries are soft and the mixture is thick, stirring occasionally with a wooden spoon.
2. Allow the mixture to cool, then store it in the plastic container for up to 2 weeks in the refrigerator.

ARE YOU NUTS ABOUT NUTS?
You can add 55g/2oz/½cup of chopped walnuts or pecans to the sauce once it is cool.

TURKEY SANDWICH

Here's an easy way to use up turkey leftovers. You can make your own cranberry sauce using the recipe above or buy it from the supermarket.

Serves: 1

YOU'LL NEED	INGREDIENTS
Chopping board	2 slices bread
Dinner knife	A little butter
Spoon	A few slices cooked turkey
Bread knife	1 slice cooked crispy bacon (optional)
	1–2 tbsp cranberry sauce
	A few lettuce or watercress leaves

1. Place the bread on a chopping board and, using a dinner knife, spread one side of each slice with butter.
2. Place the turkey and bacon, if using, on top of one slice of bread. Spoon on the cranberry sauce and top with the lettuce or watercress. Put the other slice of bread on top to form a sandwich. Cut in half with a bread knife and serve.

ADD THE STUFFING!
Instead of the bacon, you can use some leftover stuffing – heat 2 tbsp of stuffing in the microwave on high for 30 seconds before adding it on top of the cranberry sauce.

Hannukah, or festival of lights, is a Jewish holiday that occurs in mid- to late December and lasts 8 days and nights. A candle on the menorah is lit each night of Hanukah with a servant candle. These cookies are a favorite during Hannukah.

RUGELACH

These are often made with fillings. Dried fruit and nuts are as popular as chocolate. This is a delicious, yet simple sugar and spice version.

Makes: 24

YOU'LL NEED	INGREDIENTS
Oven mitts	115g/4oz/½cup butter
Measuring equipment	150g/5oz/1¼cups all-purpose flour
Dinner knife	115g/4oz/½cup cream cheese
Food processor	2 tbsp soured cream
Plastic wrap	4 tbsp superfine sugar
Small bowl	2 tsp ground cinnamon
Wooden spoon	2 tbsp butter
Small saucepan	
Rolling pin	
Pastry brush	
Baking sheet	
Cooling rack	

DREIDEL GAME!
This child's game uses a four-sided top with letters. Look for a driedel with instructions. Play spin the top and try to win objects donated by each player – these are usually nuts or chocolate coins.

1. Using a dinner knife, cut the butter into cubes. Place it in the food processor with the flour, cream cheese, and soured cream, and whiz until the mixture forms a soft dough.
2. Divide the dough into two, wrap it in plastic wrap and chill for 2 hours.
3. Combine the sugar and cinnamon in a small bowl, using a wooden spoon. Melt the butter in a small saucepan.
4. Roll each piece of dough into a 23cm/9in circle. Brush each circle generously with the melted butter and sprinkle the spicy sugar mixture on top.
5. Cut each circle into 12 wedges. Roll up the wedges, starting at the wide end, so that you end up with the point on the outside of the cookie. Place the cookies on a baking sheet and chill for 30 minutes.
6. Preheat the oven to 180°C/350°F/Gas mark 4. Bake the cookies for 20 to 25 minutes, until they are a pale golden color.
7. Cool the cookies on the baking sheet for 5 minutes before transferring to a wire rack to cool completely.

For **Christmas Pudding Sweets** turn to pages **46–47**. **Spicy Christmas Cookies** are on pages **48–49**.

Christmas

Chocolaty Log, Christmas Pudding Candies, & Spicy Christmas Cookies

Happy Christmas! There are many symbols of Christmas time, from Santa Claus and his reindeer, and nativity scenes to Christmas trees and holly. In France this log-shaped cake is called *'Buche de Noel'*, or Christmas log, and is a sign that it is Christmas time.

CHOCOLATY LOG

If you can make simple cakes, try this challenging recipe. Roll the log while the cake is still hot. Don't worry if it cracks – you can cover the cracks with icing.

Serves: 8

YOU'LL NEED

- Oven mitts
- Measuring equipment
- 33x23cm/13x9in Swiss roll tin
- Greaseproof paper or baking parchment
- Oil/pastry brush or butter for greasing
- Large mixing bowl
- Electric mixer
- Sieve
- Spatula or metal spoon
- Cook's knife
- Cooling rack
- Medium heatproof bowl
- Small saucepan
- Wooden spoon
- Small mixing bowl
- Palette knife
- Cake board or plate
- Fork

INGREDIENTS

- 4 eggs
- 115g/4oz/½cup superfine sugar, plus extra to dust
- 85g/3oz/¾cup all-purpose flour
- ½ tsp baking powder
- 3 tbsp cocoa powder

For the filling:

- 200g/7oz plain chocolate
- 115g/4oz/½cup butter
- 2 tbsp cocoa powder
- 150g/5oz/1¼cups confectioners' sugar, plus extra to sprinkle

1. Preheat the oven to 200°C/400°F/Gas mark 6. Grease and line the Swiss roll tin.
2. In the large bowl, whisk the eggs and superfine sugar together, using an electric mixer, until light and fluffy and it trails from the mixer.
3. Sift the flour, baking powder and cocoa over the mixture and gently fold in with a spatula or metal spoon. Pour it into the tin and bake for 12 to 15 minutes, until springy to the touch.
4. Meanwhile, place a sheet of baking parchment on the work surface and sprinkle lightly with superfine sugar. Turn the cake out on to the parchment and quickly and carefully peel off the lining paper and trim the edges of the cake.
5. Make a small cut about halfway through, 2.5cm/1in in from a short end. Roll up the cake from this end, with the fresh parchment inside the roll. Allow the cake to cool.
6. To make the filling, melt the chocolate in the heatproof bowl in the microwave on 50% power for 2 to 3 minutes or over a pan of gently simmering hot water. Allow it to cool.
7. Using a wooden spoon, beat the butter until pale and fluffy, then gradually beat in the cocoa powder and confectioners' sugar, followed by the cooled chocolate.
8. Unroll the cake, remove the paper and spread one-third of the filling on the cake. Re-roll it loosely and transfer to a board or long plate.
9. Spread the remaining filling on the roll, using a fork to make lines on the log. Chill the cake until the filling sets. Sprinkle with confectioners' sugar. You can decorate with artificial holly if you like.

CHRISTMAS PUDDING CANDIES

These fun-to-make sweets look like the Christmas plum puddings traditionally served after Christmas dinner in Britain.

Makes: about 20

YOU'LL NEED

- Measuring equipment
- Medium heatproof bowl
- Small saucepan
- Wooden spoon
- Baking sheet
- Sieve
- Small mixing bowl
- Metal spoon

INGREDIENTS

- 55g/2oz plain chocolate
- Small knob butter
- 1 tbsp milk
- 175g/6oz/2cups cake crumbs
- 30g/1oz/¼cup confectioners' sugar

For the frosting:

- 30g/1oz confectioners' sugar
- Yellow food coloring
- About 1 tsp water

LUCKY COIN!
Traditionally, a Christmas pudding is baked with a coin in the middle. A threepenny bit or sixpence was originally used, but today tenpence is common. Whoever finds the coin in his pudding will have good luck.

1. Break the chocolate into squares, and put it and the butter and milk in the heatproof bowl over a saucepan of hot water and stir until melted. Remove from the heat. Or heat the bowl in the microwave on 50% power for 1 to 2 minutes, then stir until combined.
2. Stir in the cake crumbs and confectioners' sugar and beat until well combined.
3. Take small pieces of the mixture and roll them into balls. If the mixture is too soft, chill it for 10 to 15 minutes before making the balls. Place the balls on the baking sheet and chill until firm.
4. To make the "custard" frosting, sift the confectioners' sugar into the small mixing bowl and add a ffew drops of yellow food coloring. Stir in just enough water, a teaspoon at a time, to make a smooth frosting – you will not need very much.
5. Drizzle the frosting over the puddings and allow it to set before serving.

TIP!
These candies make a yummy Christmas gift. Put each one in a small cupcake or muffin liner. Decorate a box with festive Christmas wrapping paper and put the candies inside so that they fit snugly together. You can add a ribbon or bow if you like or a bit of holly.

SPICY CHRISTMAS COOKIES

Traditional Christmas cookies make a great gift for friends, and they look fabulous tied with ribbon to the tree.

Makes: About 20, depending on the size of the cookie cutters.

YOU'LL NEED

- Oven gloves
- 2 baking sheets
- A little oil or butter for greasing
- 2 pastry brushes
- Large mixing bowl
- Sieve
- Dinner knife
- Fork
- Small bowl
- Wooden spoon
- Rolling pin
- Christmas cookie cutters
- Small bowl
- Cooling rack

INGREDIENTS

- 225g/8oz/2cups all-purpose flour
- ½ tsp baking powder
- 2 tsp ground mixed spice, ginger, or cinnamon
- 115g/4oz/½cup butter
- 85g/3oz/⅓cup superfine sugar
- 1 egg
- 1 small egg white
- 85g/3oz/¾cup confectioners' sugar

1. Preheat the oven to 180°C/350°F/Gas mark 4. Lightly grease two baking sheets.
2. Sift the flour, baking powder, and spice into a mixing bowl. Cut the butter into small cubes with a dinner knife and rub them into the flour with your fingertips until the mixture resembles breadcrumbs.
3. Lightly beat the egg with a fork. Stir in the sugar with a wooden spoon, then add the beaten egg mixture to the flour mixture and mix to form a soft dough.
4. Sprinkle the work surface with a little flour and roll out the dough until 6mm/¼in thick. Cut out shapes with the cookie cutters. Put the cookies slightly spaced apart on the baking sheets. Bake for 10 minutes, until pale golden.
5. Meanwhile, beat together the egg white and icing sugar with a fork. Using a pastry brush, brush the mixture over the tops of the cookies – take care as the trays will be hot. Return them to the oven for 5 minutes, until crisp and golden. Transfer to a wire rack to cool.

DECORATING THE TREE

The tradition of bringing an evergreen tree indoors at Christmas time first appeared in Germany. You can decorate your own Christmas tree like an early traditional one by using apples, nuts, cookies, and popcorn. Pine cones tied to ribbons will also make nice decorations.

TIP!

If you want to hang the cookies on a Christmas tree, make a hole in the top of each cookie with a skewer before baking them. Once the cookies have cooled, thread them on ribbons and hang on the tree. The cookies will last for up to 1 week.

2

SCHOOL'S OUT

You don't have to wait for a special celebration to have fun with your family and friends. Here are some great recipes and party suggestions for ways to have fun or simply relax on weekends or during the school vacations.

For **Crunchy Cannon Balls & Mixed Bean Salad** turn to page **54 and 55**

Summer Picnic

Tomato Soup, Crunchy Cannon Balls, & Mixed Bean Salad

Outdoor fun. When packing up for your picnic don't forget to include a blanket to sit on and plates, cups, forks, spoons, and your favorite drink. If your plans for a picnic on a nice sunny day are spoiled by rain, you can still have your picnic indoors. Spread out your picnic blanket on the floor and enjoy!

TOMATO SOUP

This fresh soup is ideal for a picnic lunch as it is delicious served cold. On cooler days you can serve the soup hot – simply store it in a vacuum flask. Make sure you use really ripe, flavorful tomatoes.

Serves: 4

YOU'LL NEED	INGREDIENTS
Measuring equipment	8 medium tomatoes
Cook's knife	4 scallions
Chopping board	450ml/15fl oz/2cups chicken or vegetable broth
Food processor	A few fresh basil leaves
Saucepan (optional)	2 tbsp sun-dried tomato paste
	Salt and freshly ground black pepper
	½ tsp superfine sugar

1. Cut the tomatoes into quarters. Then trim the scallions and slice them.
2. Place all the ingredients in a food processor and whiz for a few seconds.
3. Chill the soup until you will need it. You can store it in the refrigerator for up to 3 days.
4. If you want to serve the soup hot, on the morning of the picnic, heat it gently in a saucepan until piping hot, stirring occasionally. Then carefully pour it into the flask, which will keep it hot for several hours.

FULL OF FLAVOR!
Use tomatoes still attached to the vine for the best flavor.

Summer Picnic continued

CRUNCHY CANNON BALLS

Serves: 4

YOU'LL NEED

- Oven mitts
- Measuring equipment
- Large mixing bowl
- 2 plates
- Baking sheet
- A little oil for greasing
- Pastry brush

INGREDIENTS

- 340g/12oz lean ground pork
- 2 tbsp fresh white breadcrumbs
- 2 tbsp grated cheese, such as Cheddar, Mozzarella or Monterey Jack
- 1 egg yolk
- 1 tsp dried sage
- Salt and freshly ground black pepper
- 30g/1oz/1cup cornflakes

1. Preheat the oven to 200°C/400°F/Gas mark 6.
2. Place the meat, breadcrumbs, cheese, egg yolk, and sage in a mixing bowl and season with salt and pepper.
3. Using your fingers, squish the meat mixture together until all the ingredients are mixed. Roll the mixture into 16 to 20 small balls and place them on a plate.
4. Crush the cornflakes between the 2 plates. Roll the pork balls in the crushed cornflakes.
5. Arrange the balls on a lightly oiled baking sheet and bake for 20 minutes. Allow them to cool, then chill until cold before packing them. You can store the balls in the fridge for up to 2 days.

MIXED BEAN SALAD

Serves: 4

YOU'LL NEED

- Measuring equipment
- Cook's knife
- Chopping board
- Small saucepan
- Colander
- Large mixing bowl
- Teaspoon
- Small screw-top jar
- Large spoon

INGREDIENTS

- 150g/5oz/1cup green beans
- 400g/14oz tin red kidney beans
- 285g/10oz tin flageolet beans
- 285g/10oz tin cannellini beans
- 10 cherry tomatoes
- ⅓ cucumber
- 1 small yellow pepper

For the dressing:

- 2 tbsp olive oil
- 3 tbsp sherry vinegar
- 1 tsp whole-grain mustard
- Salt and freshly ground black pepper

1. Trim the ends off the green beans. Add the beans to a saucepan of boiling water. Cook for 3 minutes after the water begins to boil again. Drain and cool the beans under cold running water. Drain them again and place in the bowl.
2. Drain the tinned beans and rinse under cold water, using the colander, and add to the bowl.
3. Cut the cherry tomatoes in half. Cut the cucumber in half lengthways and scoop out the seeds with a teaspoon and discard them. Cut the cucumber pieces in half lengthways again, then thickly slice. Remove the core and seeds from the pepper and cut it into small pieces. Add these vegetables to the bowl.
4. Place the ingredients for the dressing in the jar. Screw on the lid and shake well. Pour over the salad and mix well with a large spoon.

FRUITY OAT BARS

Makes: 8

1. Place the cranberries or sultanas and apple juice in the small saucepan and heat gently until the juice just begins to bubble. Turn off the heat and leave for 1 hour to let the fruit soften.

2. Preheat the oven to 170°C/325°F/Gas mark 3. Lightly grease the baking pan with the oil or butter, trim the lining paper with the scissors and line the base of the tin.

3. Place the butter, sugar, and honey in the large saucepan and heat gently, stirring until the butter melts and the sugar dissolves. Remove the pan from the heat and place it carefully on a heatproof surface.

4. Carefully stir in the sultanas, oats, seeds, and flour and mix until thoroughly combined – the mixture and pan will be very hot.

5. Spoon the mixture into the tin and level it. Bake for 20 to 25 minutes until pale golden.

6. While still hot, carefully cut the baked oatmeal mixture into 8 bars, then allow them to cool in the baking tin for 5 minutes before transferring them to a wire rack to cool completely.

YOU'LL NEED	INGREDIENTS
Oven mitts Small saucepan 18cm/7in square baking pan Greaseproof paper or nonstick baking parchment Scissors Oil/pastry brush or butter for greasing Large saucepan Wooden spoon Cook's knife Cooling rack	115g/4oz/⅔cup dried cranberries or sultanas 3 tbsp apple juice 115g/4oz/½cup butter 4 tbsp light muscovado sugar 2 tbsp clear honey 150g/5oz/1¼cups oatmeal 30g/1oz/¼cup sesame seeds or linseeds 3 tbsp wholewheat flour

You'll find the recipes for **Carrot Cupcakes & Ultimate Hot Chocolate** on pages **58–59.**

Slumber Party

Greek Pitta Pockets, Carrot Cupcakes, & Ultimate Hot Chocolate

Planning the night. Make the Carrot Cupcakes before your guests arrive, but they can help you make the Greek Pitta Pockets. Plan some other activities such as making friendship bracelets that you can exchange and perhaps a game such as Twister. Don't forget to supply a torch or two for bedtime fun.

GREEK PITTA POCKETS

This is a great supper that can be made in minutes and enjoyed in front of the TV or sitting on the floor having a good gossip.

Serves: 4

YOU'LL NEED	INGREDIENTS
Measuring equipment	⅓ medium cucumber
Cook's knife	6 cherry tomatoes
Chopping board	½ red bell pepper
Teaspoon	150g/5oz feta cheese
Large mixing bowl	8 cos lettuce leaves
Large spoon	½ small red onion
Small bowl	8 pitted black olives
Fork	***For the dressing:***
	2 tbsp olive oil
	2 tsp lemon juice
	Ground black pepper
	4 pitta breads

1. Cut the cucumber in half, scoop out the seeds with a teaspoon and cut it into chunks. Cut the cherry tomatoes in half. Remove and discard the core and seeds of the pepper and cut it into bite-sized pieces.
2. Cut the cheese into small cubes and cut the lettuce into thick slices. Cut a few thin slices from the red onion.
3. Toss together the cucumber, tomato, pepper, cheese, lettuce leaves, onion and olives (you can leave these out if you don't like olives) in a mixing bowl.
4. In the small bowl whisk together the olive oil, lemon juice and pepper with a fork, and pour the dressing over the salad. Toss it lightly to coat the salad.
5. Split open the pitta breads and fill each one with one-quarter of the salad. The sandwiches are now ready to be served.

PUFFY BREAD!
Heat the pitta breads before splitting them open – they will puff up.

Slumber Party continued

CARROT CUPCAKES

Makes: 12

YOU'LL NEED

- Oven mitts
- Measuring equipment
- Mixing bowl
- Hand-held electric mixer or wooden spoon
- Grater
- A muffin tray lined with 12 paper cases
- Small metal spoon
- Cooling rack
- Small bowl
- Wooden spoon
- Dinner knife

INGREDIENTS

- 85g/3oz/6 tbsp butter, softened
- 85g/3oz/⅓cup light muscovado sugar
- 85g/3oz/¾cup wholewheat flour
- 30g/1oz/¼cup all-purpose flour
- 1 tsp baking powder
- 2 eggs
- 3 tbsp orange juice
- 1 large carrot
- 55g/2oz/⅓cup sultanas

For the topping:

- 115g/4oz low-fat cream cheese
- 4 tsp honey or maple syrup

1. Preheat the oven to 180°C/350°F/Gas mark 4.
2. Place the butter, sugar, wholemeal and plain flours, baking powder, eggs, and orange juice in the bowl and beat until well combined.
3. Finely grate the carrot – watch out for the grater's sharp teeth. Mix in the grated carrot and sultanas. Using a small spoon, divide the mixture equally among the paper cases.
4. Bake in the center of the oven for 12 to 15 minutes, until they are golden and springy to the touch. Allow to cool in the tin for a few minutes, then transfer to a wire rack to cool completely before the next step.
5. For the topping beat the cheese and honey or maple syrup together until combined and spread a little over the top of each cake using a dinner knife.

TIP!
You can make these cupcakes more fun by topping them with some sugar sprinkles. Or press chocolate chips into the topping in a star or other pattern.

ULTIMATE HOT CHOCOLATE

Serves: 4

YOU'LL NEED

- Measuring equipment
- Cook's knife
- Chopping board
- Small saucepan
- Wooden spoon
- 4 mugs

INGREDIENTS

- 200g/7oz plain chocolate
- 900ml/30fl oz/3¾cups full-fat milk
- Sugar to taste
- A few marshmallows (optional)
- Cocoa powder (optional)

1. Chop the chocolate into small pieces.
2. Pour the milk into the pan and heat gently until bubbles appear around the edge of the pan, then stir in the chocolate.
3. Continue to heat, stirring constantly, until the chocolate melts and blends with the milk.
4. Pour the mixture into the mugs and add sugar until the drinks are sweet enough. Serve with a few marshmallows on top and sprinkle with a little cocoa powder if you like.

You'll find **Spicy Potato Skins** on pages **62-63**

Chill Out Saturdays

Chicken Nuggets & Spicy Potato Skins

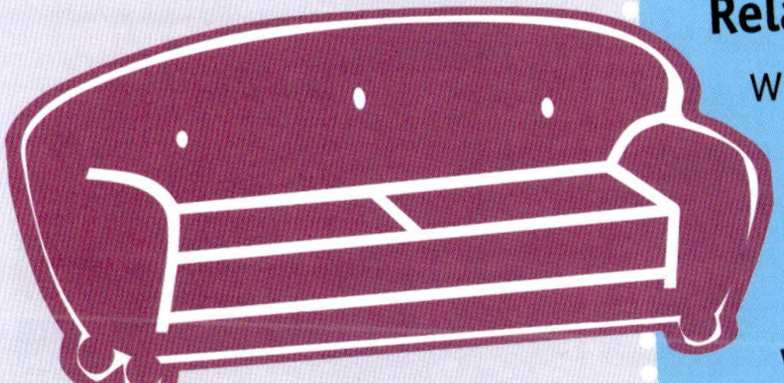

Relax. After a long week at school and with a busy weekend ahead, take time out to refuel with these laid-back snacks. They are fun to make – and they are even more fun to eat if you invite over a few friends to help make them disappear while watching your favorite program on TV.

CHICKEN NUGGETS

These are easy to make – and your parents will be happy because they are more nutritious and lower in fat than shop-bought nuggets. Serve them with Spicy Potato Skins and a green salad for a meal.

Serves: 4

YOU'LL NEED	INGREDIENTS
Oven mitts	4 skinless, boneless chicken breasts
Measuring equipment	1 egg
Baking sheet	55g/2oz/½cup dried breadcrumbs
Pastry brush	4 tbsp sesame seeds
Cook's knife for raw meat	2 tbsp all-purpose flour
Chopping board	1 tsp paprika
Spoon	2 tbsp sunflower oil extra for greasing
Small bowl	
Fork	
2 plates	

1. Preheat the oven to 200°C/400°F/Gas mark 6. Lightly brush a baking sheet with a little oil.
2. Carefully cut the chicken crosswise into strips.
3. Lightly beat the egg with the fork in a bowl. Combine the breadcrumbs and sesame seeds together on a plate. Mix the flour and paprika together on another plate.
4. Dust the chicken strips with the flour, then dip in the egg before coating with the sesame seed mixture.
5. Lay out the chicken strips on the oiled baking sheet. Drizzle with the oil.
6. Bake the chicken in the center of the oven for 15 to 20 minutes or until crisp and golden, turning once.

A YUMMY DIP!
If you are serving these and the Spicy Potato Skins with salsa, try dipping the nuggets in the salsa too!

SPICY POTATO SKINS

These potato skins get their scrumptious texture from being baked in the oven twice. They are also the perfect choice for a get-together if you or any of your friends are vegetarian.

Serves: 4

YOU'LL NEED	INGREDIENTS
Oven mitts	3 large baking potatoes
Fork	4 tbsp olive oil
Baking sheet	1 clove garlic
Measuring equipment	1 tsp paprika
Cook's knife	½ tsp chilli powder
Chopping board	¼ tsp each ground cumin and coriander
Spoon	
Garlic press	***To serve:***
Small bowls	Soured cream, salsa, or ketchup
Pastry brush	

FISHY LEFTOVERS!
Use the leftover potato flesh to make these easy fish cakes. Mash the potato, then add a little butter and milk and mix together. Add some flaked tuna fish, form patties and fry until golden.

1. Preheat the oven to 220°C/425°F/Gas mark 7. Scrub the potatoes and prick them all over with a fork and place on a baking sheet. Bake the potatoes for 1 hour until soft and remove them from the oven, but leave the oven on.

2. Allow the potatoes to cool. Then cut into quarters and scoop out the flesh, but leave a small amount still attached the skin. Keep the leftover potato flesh in a container to use another time. Cut each potato skin in half.

3. Peel and crush the garlic. In a small bowl, mix together the oil, garlic, and spices with a fork. Brush the spicy oil over both sides of the potato skins and arrange in a single layer on a baking sheet.

4. Bake the potato skins for 15 to 20 minutes until they are crisp.

5. Serve the potato skins with soured cream, salsa or ketchup in a small bowl for dipping. Or serve all the condiments in separate bowls and let your friends choose their favorite dip.

MAKE IT FILLING!
You can top the potato skins with Cheddar or Monterey Jack cheese before putting them in the oven – or try stuffing them with onions, peppers, and mushrooms fried for 5 minutes.

Index